A Taste of
Chicken Soup for the

Dog Lover's
Soul®

Stories of Canine Companionship, Comedy
and Courage

Jack Canfield, Mark Victor Hansen,
Marty Becker, D.V.M., Carol Kline,
Amy D. Shojai

Chicken Soup for the Soul Publishing, LLC
Cos Cob, CT

A Taste of Chicken Soup for the Dog Lover's Soul®
Stories of Canine Companionship, Comedy and Courage
Jack Canfield, Mark Victor Hansen, Marty Becker, Carol Kline and
Amy D. Shojai

Published by Chicken Soup for the Soul Publishing, LLC
www.chickensoup.com

Copyright © 2013 by Chicken Soup for the Soul Publishing, LLC.
All Rights Reserved. No part of this publication may be reproduced,
stored in a retrieval system or transmitted in any form or by
any means, electronic, mechanical, photocopying, recording or
otherwise, without the written permission of the publisher.

CSS, Chicken Soup for the Soul, and its Logo and Marks are
trademarks of Chicken Soup for the Soul Publishing, LLC
The publisher gratefully acknowledges the many publishers
and individuals who granted Chicken Soup for the Soul
permission to reprint the cited material.

Front cover ©2005 Best Friends/Troy Snow

Library of Congress Control Number: 2013944000

Taste of ISBN: 978-1-61159-862-9

Full Book ISBN: 978-1-62361-034-0

Contents

Moving Day, *Micki Ruiz*......................................1

Refrigerator Commando, *Sam Minier*............8

A Canine Nanny, *Christine Henderson*...........14

Abacus, *Meghan Beeby*.......................................19

A New Home, *Elisabeth A. Freeman*...............27

The Last Puppy, *Roger Dean Kiser*.................36

Scouting Out a Home, *Jennifer Coates,*
    D.V.M...43

The Parking-Lot Dog, *Wendy Kaminsky*.........52

The Promise, *Bill King*.....................................59

Sled Dogs Without Snow, *Dave Wiley*...........69

About Our Contributors....................................76

Meet Our Authors...80

About Chicken Soup for the Soul...................89

Moving Day

He was a street dog of indeterminable pedigree. Not too big, but scrappy.

He found my husband on St. Patrick's Day, 1988. A New York City police officer, Steve was patrolling the Park Slope section of Brooklyn. The skinny blond dog with the white stripe on his face and stand-up ears he never did grow into, fairly leaped into the patrol car through the open window.

I got the call that afternoon. "Can we keep him?" My big strong husband sounded like a kid.

We kept him. Steve named him Patrick, in honor of the day he'd found him. We didn't know how he'd ended up a homeless pup. But it didn't matter. He was safe now. The vet estimated that he was about six months old and that he'd been on the streets only a few days. He was healthy, but awfully hungry.

I fed him boiled chicken and rice, easy on his stomach, and determined to start putting some meat on the ribs that were a bit too prominent. After that meal—and after every single meal I fed him for the rest of his life— he thanked me with several sloppy kisses on my hands.

Things were hectic that March. The kids were growing and we were in the process of moving into a larger apartment.

Patrick watched with an odd expression; but it was an odd move. We didn't really pack. We simply rolled everything into the hall, loaded it in the elevator, went two floors down and rolled the stuff off and into the new place.

The new apartment gave our kids their own rooms. Patrick's space was an alcove at the end of the hall leading to the master bedroom. I cut a piece of carpet to fit his "room" and piled his toys in one of the corners. I bought "Dawn Lane" and "Michael Lane" signs for the kids, so of course I bought a "Patrick Lane" sign for him. I think he liked it. When I put it on the wall he licked the sign, then me.

March 17 became his birthday. On the first anniversary of the day he found us, I threw a "Patty Party," inviting all the grandparents. I'd done it tongue-in-cheek, but it became an annual event. We got Patrick a kelly-green birthday hat and a big matching bow tie. Another dog might have been embarrassed; Patrick wore them with pride.

To repay us for rescuing him, Patrick protected us with zeal and an unerring ability to tell good guy from bad. He could pick the "perp" out of a lineup a block long. He knew guns, too. When Steve cleaned his service revolver, Patrick would eye him strangely, from a safe distance, as if to say, "What's a nice guy like you doing with a thing like that?"

In 1992 Steve retired. We bought a house in

Jersey near my folks, but couldn't close until October. The kids stayed with my parents so they could start the year in their new school. We brought them home on alternate weekends. Michael's room now became the "Box Room."

Every day I knelt in that room, placing breakables on the pile of papers, wrapping them up and tucking them into boxes. And every day Patrick watched from the room's other doorway. I told him all about "our" new house and described the fun "we" would have.

Our last night in Brooklyn approached. We'd lived in that apartment four and a half years, and in the building for fifteen. Though excited about moving into our own home, we were a bit sad to leave the city we'd lived in all our lives. Patrick understood. He patrolled the apartment restlessly, sniffing every nook and cranny as if to commit to memory the security of the only loving home he'd ever known.

We closed on the house on Friday, then drove back to Brooklyn with the kids. The

"Box Room" was nearly full, but the packing paper still lay on the few square feet of remaining floor, ready to protect our last-minute treasures. I gave the kids their "Dawn" and "Michael" boxes, instructing them to finish packing their toys. We had something quick for dinner. I don't remember what. I only remember what happened after.

I walked into the kitchen and happened to glance into the "Box Room." I was stunned.

"Hey, guys," I called. "You won't believe what Patrick did." They followed me through the kitchen. Patrick poked his nose in from the living-room doorway, a very worried expression on his face.

There, nestled in the canyon of cartons, lying right on top of the newspaper used for wrapping breakables, was Patrick's favorite toy.

I said, "Patty, are you afraid we're going to move away and leave you? Is that what those other people did to you?" He didn't need words. His eyes told me.

"Well," I told him. "You don't have to worry. We're not going to leave you. You're coming with us."

Then I rolled up his toy in the paper. I'd planned to put his things in the "Patrick" box. Instead, it went in with our dishes. It seemed the thing to do.

His bushy blond and white tail wagged like mad, and if asked under oath I'd have to swear he laughed. We all wound up in a heap on that stack of papers, getting licked to death by one very happy—and grateful—dog.

I'm sorry to say I'd never considered Patrick's feelings through that whole tumultuous process; never thought he was worried as he sat day after day, intently watching me wrap up and pack away our things; never realized he didn't know he was part of the "we" I kept mentioning. After all, he'd been with us four and a half years and we'd moved with him before. But I guess the vast amount of packing required for this move dredged up old memories and threatened his sense of security.

Elephants never forget; dogs don't either.

When I think about Patty now, all I can say is: I'm thrilled he picked Steve. He brought joy to our lives that we would have sorely missed otherwise. He left us in November 1997 and we still miss him. He's with us, though, in a pretty wooden urn—and he smiles at us every day from his picture, dressed so smartly in his kelly-green birthday hat and matching bow tie.

~Micki Ruiz

Refrigerator Commando

A golden barrel on legs—that was our first impression of Max when my wife and I saw him at the Animal Welfare League. His unique ability to inhale a full cup of dog food in less than seven seconds had enabled Max to enlarge his beagle-mix body into the shape of an overstuffed sausage. Even after Heather and I adopted him and helped him lose weight, we were continually amazed at his voraciousness. His escapades became the stuff of family legend: his seek-and-destroy mission involving several pounds of gourmet Christmas cashews, his insistence on chasing birds away from the feeder so *he* could eat the seeds, his discovery (far too gross to discuss here) of the yeasty joys of Amish Friendship Bread batter. And of course the refrigerator story . . .

One day during her lunch break, Heather called me at work. "Did you shut the refrigerator door tight this morning?"

"Think so. Why?"

She paused just enough to let the suspense build. "Max raided the fridge."

We got off lucky: we were overdue to go to the grocery store, so there hadn't been much in there. He'd gotten the last couple of pieces of peppered turkey and maybe a third of a bag of baby carrots—no surprise there, Max loves carrots (then again, Max loves potting soil). Still, no real damage done. We wrote it off to a sloppily closed door (probably my doing), and the next morning I made sure everything was shut good and tight before I left. After all, we had just loaded up with groceries the night before, and we wouldn't want my carelessness to help Max get himself into trouble, right?

Turns out Max didn't need my help at all.

Again a phone call to me during Heather's

lunch hour, this time straight to the point: "I think he knows how to open the refrigerator," she said.

"What?!"

Max had made himself a sandwich. A *big* sandwich: a pound of turkey, a pound of Swiss cheese, a head of lettuce, half a tomato and an entire loaf of bread. He'd also ripped open another bag of carrots and polished off the remnants of a bag of shredded coconut (for dessert, I assume). Heather found him lying amid the flurry of destroyed plastic bags, tail desperately thumping at her displeasure, as if to say, *Please don't be mad, it was just* SOOOO *good* . . .

Still, we didn't really believe it. He couldn't reach the handle, and the door seal was tight. How was he doing it? I caught him that night, after putting away our second load of groceries in two days. I just happened to be passing by the darkened kitchen when I saw his stout little body wiggling, pushing his narrow muzzle into the fridge seal like a wedge. Then, with a quick flick of his head, he popped the door open.

Apparently, Max, while not understanding the gastrointestinal distress that results from eating sixteen slices of cheese, had a full understanding of the concept of the lever. Where was this dog when I'd been in science class?

This was serious. He now had the skill, the determination and, most important, the appetite to literally eat us out of house and home. The next morning, as a temporary fix, we blocked the refrigerator with a heavy toolbox. Surely he couldn't move a barrier loaded with close to twenty-five pounds of metal, could he?

Another lunchtime phone call. I think I answered it: "You've got to be kidding!"

The moving of the toolbox still remains a bit of a mystery. I'm guessing he used that lever principle again, wedging his muzzle between the box and the door and then just pushing for all he was worth. And once that barrier was gone, he got *serious*.

More bread, more meat, more cheese. The

rest of the carrots. Apples—many, many apples. A packet of cilantro, smeared like green confetti across the kitchen floor. He'd also popped open a Tupperware bowl of angel hair pasta and had been working at its sister container of tomato sauce when Heather found him. The only items left on the bottom two shelves were beer and pop, and the only thing that saved those was his lack of opposable thumbs.

That night we decided to hit the grocery store for a *third* time and invest in a childproof lock for the fridge. Before we left the house to buy it, we hovered anxiously around the refrigerator for a while. There wasn't *much* left in there, but still, what if he tried to climb to the top shelves? What if he conquered the freezer?

But what could stop him? The toolbox had been no match. Finally, I half lifted, half dragged the seventy-five-pound safe from my office closet, dragged it to the kitchen and thudded it onto the floor, flush against the door.

Max sat behind us, watching. Calculating.

Heather leaned into me, almost whispering. "Do you think it will work?"

I said, "Well, I think we'll find one of three things when we get back. One, everything will be fine. Two, the safe will be budged a couple inches, and we'll have a beagle with a very red and throbbing nose. Or three, we may come home and find he's rigged up some elaborate pulley system that's lifted the safe out of his way. If that's the case, I say from now on, we just stock the bottom two shelves with whatever he wants."

We dashed to the store and back in record time. We practically ran into the kitchen and found him lying there, thinking deeply. No sore nose, no pulley system. We sighed big sighs of relief and got the plastic and vinyl childproof strap installed. So far it's done its job. So far . . .

~Sam Minier

A Canine Nanny

I was physically and emotionally exhausted. At night, I was awake more than I slept, caring for our three-week-old daughter, Abigail. By day, I chased our older daughter, Bridget, an active two-year-old. My already taut nerves began to fray when Abigail developed a mild case of colic. Bridget demanded attention each time her sister fussed. Our dog, a purebred Brittany named Two, was constantly underfoot, and stumbling over her repeatedly did not help my state of mind.

I also felt isolated. We were new to the area, and I didn't know anyone in town. My parents, our nearest relatives, lived 150 miles away. Phoning my mother on the spur of the moment to ask if she'd drop by and watch the kids for an hour while I got some much-needed sleep wasn't realistic. My husband helped as much as he could but needed to focus on his job.

One day Abigail woke from a nap. As babies sometimes do, she had soiled her clothing and crib bedding. I tried to clean her up as fast as possible, but her cries developed into ear-shattering wails before I was through. I wanted to comfort her, but I was at a loss. I had to wash my hands, I couldn't put her back into the crib and the floor hadn't been vacuumed for days. Strapping her on the changing table, I wedged a receiving blanket between her and the railing. I promised I'd be right back. As her screams followed me into the bathroom, I neared complete meltdown. Women had handled this for generations—why couldn't I cope?

I had just lathered up with soap when Two trotted purposefully past the bathroom door. A moment later the crying ceased. Hurriedly,

I dried my hands and entered the nursery to find the Brittany standing on her hind legs, tenderly licking Abigail's ear. The baby's eyes were opened wide in wonder. Two dropped down and wagged her stubby tail in apology. With a canine grin and her ears pushed back as far as they could go, she seemed to say, "I know babies are off limits, but I couldn't help myself."

At that moment, I realized why I had been tripping over Two all the time: she wanted to help! When Bridget was born, Two had enthusiastically welcomed the newest member of her family. But because she had difficulty curbing her energy, we had watched her closely. Now, at six years of age, with a more sedate disposition, Two understood she had to be gentle.

That day marked a turning point for me. During Abigail's fussy moments, I laid her blanket on the floor and placed her next to Two. Often Abigail quieted as she buried her hands and feet in the dog's warm soft fur.

Although Two relished her role as babysitter, objecting only when Abigail grabbed a fistful of sensitive flank hair, I still kept a vigilant eye on them, or Abigail would likely have suffered a constant barrage of doggy kisses.

When Abigail turned four, we enrolled her in preschool. Her teacher as well as several of the other parents commented on how she was always the child who reached out to those who were alone. Extending an invitation to join in play, Abigail often stayed by someone's side if she didn't get an answer, talking quietly and reassuringly. I like to think that Two's willingness to remain lying next to a screaming infant somehow contributed to our daughter's sensitivity.

I admit I've spoiled Two since that first day when she comforted Abigail. If I leave the table and a half-eaten meal disappears, I know who the culprit is. But I don't have the heart to punish her for being an opportunist. I'm indebted to her, and losing out on several bites of cold food is a small price to pay.

Two is still part of our family, and although we all dote on her, there is an unmistakable connection between her and Abigail. Now nearly twelve years old, Two has more than her share of aches and pains. During winter, she often rests in front of the heat register. When Abigail wakes in the morning, she covers *her* dog with her old baby blanket and fusses over her. And when Abigail wanders away, Two trails after her, the tattered blanket dragging along on the floor. Two still considers Abigail her special charge, and I'm happy to have her help. I hope they have many more days together, looking after each other with such loving care.

~Christine Henderson

Abacus

A lot has been written about what dogs can do for people. Dogs lead the blind, aid the deaf, sniff out illegal substances, give us therapeutic hope and joy, make us laugh with their idiosyncrasies, and give us companionship—to name just a few of their many talents. But what about our duty to dogs—what about their needs, wants, hopes and joys? And what about the ones most people do not want to adopt— the ones who aren't completely healthy or cute? This is a story of just such a dog.

I first learned about Abacus while doing some Internet research on special-needs dogs. I had become interested in special-needs dogs after losing my brother Damon, who was left paraplegic after an accident in 1992 and committed suicide three years later. Damon loved exploring the outdoors and preferred the freedom of driving a truck to working behind a desk all day. Losing those options was difficult enough for him, but the thought that nobody would want him was more than he could deal with. His death made me more aware of the challenges that people—and animals—with disabilities must face.

I knew my husband and I couldn't get a dog because of the no-pets policy at our rental, but I couldn't keep myself from researching them. On *www.petfinder.com,* there was a listing for a very handsome fellow named Abacus who was staying at Animal Lifeline, a no-kill animal shelter located near Des Moines, Iowa. Abacus had originally been rescued as a stray puppy two years earlier by the kind staff at a veterinary hospital in Nebraska after being hit by a car and subsequently paralyzed. Normally, a stray dog with partial paralysis would have been euthanized because few people want to adopt a dog in that condition. But the veterinarian and his staff saw something special and endearing in Abacus. They took him under their wing and eventually entrusted the shelter in Iowa with his care.

The picture of Abacus on the shelter's Web site showed a largish black dog with a rubber ducky in a hydrotherapy tub, enjoying a workout to help improve the muscle tone in his paralyzed hind legs. Through his photograph alone, Abacus cast his spell on me and I was never the same.

I couldn't get the image of Abacus out of my mind and felt compelled to visit him—even though I knew I couldn't adopt him. My husband, John, supportive and understanding as always, drove with me on the nearly two-hour drive to the special-needs animal shelter. When I first saw Abacus in his quarters at the shelter, my breath stopped for a few seconds. It was a little disconcerting to see his atrophied hind legs, the result of his paralysis, but his exuberance and happy-go-lucky attitude quickly masked his physical challenges. I was struck by the sheer joy he radiated. His wide, loving eyes stayed in my mind and heart long after we drove away from the shelter.

Meeting Abacus inspired me to start looking for a house to buy instead of continuing to rent. Soon we found a nice rural home with acreage at an affordable price. I applied to adopt Abacus, and we were able to celebrate his third birthday by bringing him home with us a few weeks later.

Life with Abacus required a few adjustments. I learned daily therapeutic exercises for his hind legs, and how to get his strong, wiggly body into his wheelchair (called a K-9 cart) by myself. His castle, when I am not home, is a special padded room with a comfy mattress and lots of blankets and washable rugs. Often, I wrap his paralyzed legs in gauze bandages to help protect them from the abrasions he gets from dragging them on the floor or from the uncontrollable muscle spasms that occur in his hindquarters.

When Abacus is inside the house but out of his cart, he scoots around using his strong, muscular front legs. At times he can support his hind legs for a while, which looks a bit like a donkey kicking and occasionally causes him to knock things down as he maneuvers around the house. But when he is in his K-9 cart, Abacus can run like the wind. We have to supervise our canine Evel Knievel in his cart since he can tip it over and get stuck when taking curves too fast.

Even though he requires extra care, I have never thought of Abacus as a burden. Living with him is a privilege. Enthusiastic about everything, he treats strangers like long-lost friends. And as much as he loves food, he loves cuddles even more. His zest for life inspires me, as well as others who meet him. Some people who see him feel pity for his challenges, but I always point out that he is not depressed or daunted by his differentness. I am sure if Abacus could speak, he would say that special-needs dogs can live happy, full lives and can enrich the lives of their adopters as much as—if not more than—a "normal" dog can.

The main reason I adopted Abacus was because I wanted to give him the comfort and security of a forever home, but in addition to that, I felt that he could help me give encouragement to others. A principle I have always lived by was shaped by part of an Emily Dickinson poem I learned as a child:

> *If I can ease one life the aching*
> *Or cool one pain,*
> *Or help one fainting robin*
> *Unto his nest again,*
> *I shall not live in vain.*

I only wish my brother could have known Abacus. For although animal-assisted therapy is not a cure-all, I believe a seed of hope can be planted in the heart of a physically, mentally or emotionally challenged child—or adult—when he sees a special-needs animal living a full and happy life in a loving home.

To spread this hope, I worked with Abacus to train him to become a certified therapy dog. After passing an evaluation this year, Abacus has begun visiting a school for special children. My employers at Farm Sanctuary—an organization that understands the mutual healing power that people and animals share—graciously grant me permission to take time off work for these twice-monthly weekday visits. Abacus looks forward to these excursions and always wows the kids (and teachers) with his bouncy "Tigger-like" personality. On occasion, his visiting attire includes his snazzy Super Dog cape that flies behind him as he zooms around in his wheelchair. Abacus always leaves happiness in his wake.

Living with a special-needs animal isn't for everyone, but it is a rare treat for those who choose to take it on. In fact, my experience with Abacus has inspired me to adopt a number of other special-needs animals over the years. All of them have more than repaid my investment of time and energy by being constant positive reminders that life's challenges need not be met with despair and negativity. Their love is healing, their appreciation rewarding, and their quirky personalities add priceless meaning to my life.

~Meghan Beeby

A New Home

"Mom, watch out!" my daughter Melissa screamed as a drenched brown pooch charged under our van. Slamming my foot on the brakes, we jerked to a stop. Stepping out into the freezing rain, we hunched down on opposite sides of the van, making kissing noises to coax the little dog—who, miraculously, I hadn't hit—to us. The shivering pup jumped into Melissa's arms and then onto her lap once she sat down again in the heated van.

We were on our way home from Melissa's sixth-grade basketball game. Her once-white shirt with the red number 7 was now covered in dirty black paw prints. I stared at the mess as she wrapped her shirt around the small dog.

"That shirt will never come clean!"

"Well, at least we saved his life," she frowned as she cuddled him. "Running through all those cars he could have been killed."

She continued petting him. "He's so cute. And he doesn't have a collar. Can we keep him?"

I knew how she felt. I loved animals myself—especially dogs. But I also knew the mess they made. Dogs dig through the garbage. They chew up paper, shoes and anything else they can fit in their mouths. Not to mention the little piles and puddles they make when you're trying to housebreak them. I didn't need a dog. I loved the clean, bright house we had recently moved into, and I wanted to keep my new house looking just that—new.

I glanced at the ball of brown fur and the black mask outlining his wide, wondering eyes. *She's right. He is cute.*

The smell of wet dog escalated with the burst of heat coming out of the vents, bringing me to my senses. I turned the heat down and shook my head. "Melissa, we've been through this before. I told all four of you kids when we moved into the new house: absolutely no pets."

As we pulled into the drive, she said, "But Mom, it's the middle of February. He'll freeze out here."

I glanced at the pup licking Melissa's fingers. "Okay," I decided. "We'll give him a bath, keep him for the night and call the animal shelter tomorrow."

Still frowning, Melissa nodded and slid out of the van. Carrying the dog in her arms, she entered the house. By the time I reached the door, the news was already out.

"We've got a new puppy!" Robert, Brian and Jeremiah chorused.

"I'm afraid not," I said, as I took off my shoes. "We're only keeping him overnight."

Wiggling out of Melissa's arms, the pup scampered across the room and jumped up on my couch.

"Get down!" I shouted, pointing my finger at him and toward the floor.

He licked his nose remorsefully and sat there shaking.

"Mom, you're scaring him." Melissa scooped him into her arms. "C'mon, boy, I'll take you to my room."

"Ah-ah," I corrected, "bath first."

All four kids crowded around the puppy in the bathroom. I listened over the running water as each became excited over every splash the dog made. Their giggles brought a smile to my face. *Maybe it wouldn't be such a bad idea to have a dog.*

I glanced around the kitchen with its shiny black-and-white tile floor. Picturing a dog dish, with food and water heaping into a sloshing puddle of goo, I turned toward the living room. With this messy weather, I envisioned my pale-blue carpeting "decorated" with tiny black paw prints. Not to mention the shedding, fleas and all the other things a dog can bring. I shook my head. *A dog will ruin this place.*

After his bath, Melissa brought him out wrapped in one of our good white towels. He looked like a drowned rat, except for his big, brown puppy-dog eyes. The boys raced around the kitchen getting food and water.

The water sloshed back and forth in the bowl. "Be careful, Jeremiah," I warned. "You're gonna spill—" When Jeremiah heard my voice he stopped with a sudden jerk. Water splashed onto his face and down the front of shirt and blue jeans, soaking the floor.

I ran to get towels. When I returned, I watched in horror as the pup tramped through the water. Even after his bath, his feet were still dirty and left muddy little prints all over my kitchen floor. "Wipe his feet and put him in your room, Melissa. *Now!*"

Melissa snatched the dog up, with the boys traipsing at her heels. I sighed as I wiped up the mud and water. After a few minutes, the floor shined like new, and laughter erupted from Melissa's bedroom.

My husband, John, came in from work

moments later. "What's so funny?" he asked after he kissed me on the cheek.

"A dog."

"A dog?" he asked, surprised. "We have a dog?"

"Not by choice," I explained. "It ran under the van. And of course I couldn't just leave him in the middle of the street."

John smiled. "What happened to no pets?"

"I told them he's going tomorrow."

After John joined the kids he came back out. "You know, he is really cute."

"Yeah, I know." He didn't have to convince me; my resolve was already slipping.

The next morning, the kids mauled the dog with hugs and tears. "Can't we keep him?" they sobbed. I watched how he gently and tenderly licked each one as if to comfort them.

"I promise we'll take care of him," Melissa said.

"Yeah, and I'll water him," Jeremiah added. I smiled, remembering the incident the night before. "But I won't fill his dish so full next time."

How could I say no? *He's housebroken. He's cute. And he's great with the kids.*

"We'll see," I said, as they scooted out the door for school. "But first, I'll have to call the dog pound to make sure no one is looking for him."

Their faces lit up as they trotted down the drive. With John already at work, the pup and I watched from the door as the four kids skipped down the street. Once they turned the corner, I grabbed the phone book and found the number for the animal shelter.

The lady at the shelter informed me that no one had reported a brown dog missing. However, she instructed me to put an ad in the local paper about him for three days, and if no one responded, we could legally keep him for our own. I called the newspaper and placed the ad. Although I had mixed feelings, mostly I hoped his owners would claim him.

Each day, the kids would ask the same

question, "Did anyone call?" And each day it was always the same answer: "Nope."

By the third day, the dog and I had spent so much time together that he followed me around the house. If I sat on the couch, he'd jump in my lap. If I folded clothes, he'd lie by the dryer. If I made dinner, he'd sit by the refrigerator. Even when I went to bed, he'd follow, wanting to cuddle up with me.

"Looks like we have to come up with a name," I said Sunday morning at breakfast.

The kids cheered and threw out some names. When we returned from church, I played the messages on our answering machine, my heart sinking when I heard: "I think you may have my dog."

After speaking with the lady, I realized that Snickers was indeed her dog. She explained she'd be over to get him within the hour. As we sat around the table, picking at the pot roast, tears flooded our plates like a river. Even I had grown attached to this sweet little dog.

When the lady arrived, I met her at the

door. I clenched a wet tissue in my hands and invited her in. She took in the scene: four mournful children sitting in a huddle around the little dog and petting him, while Snickers, perched on Melissa's lap, licked her tears away.

After a long moment, she said, "I want you to have him. I can see you love him and we already have another dog."

I gave her a hug while the kids cheered in the background.

Snickers has definitely left his mark on our house. Still, I wouldn't trade his muddy paw prints for anything—not even the nicest-looking house in the world! For, although he makes little messes sometimes, he has filled our hearts with love. Before Snickers came into our lives, we had a new house. Now we have a new home.

~Elisabeth A. Freeman

The Last Puppy

It had been a very long night. Our black cocker spaniel, Precious, was having a difficult delivery. I lay on the floor beside her large four-foot-square cage, watching her every movement. Watching and waiting, just in case I had to rush her to the veterinarian.

After six hours the puppies started to appear. The first-born was black and white. The second and third puppies were tan and brown. The fourth and fifth were spotted black and white. *One, two, three, four, five,* I counted to myself as I walked down the hallway to wake my wife, Judy, and tell her that everything was fine.

As we walked back down the hallway and

into the spare bedroom, I noticed a sixth puppy had been born and was now lying all by itself over to the side of the cage. I picked up the small puppy and lay it on top of the large pile of puppies, who were whining and trying to nurse on the mother. Precious immediately pushed the small puppy away from rest of the group. She refused to recognize it as a member of her family.

"Something's wrong," said Judy.

I reached over and picked up the puppy. My heart sank inside my chest when I saw the puppy had a cleft lip and palate and could not close its tiny mouth. I decided right then and there that if there was any way to save this animal, I was going to give it my best shot.

I took the puppy to the vet and was told nothing could be done unless we were willing to spend about a thousand dollars to try to correct the defect. He told us that the puppy would die mainly because it could not suckle.

After returning home Judy and I decided that we could not afford to spend that kind of money without getting some type of assurance from the vet that the puppy had a chance to survive. However, that did not stop me from purchasing a syringe and feeding the puppy by hand— which I did day and night, every two hours, for more than ten days. The little puppy survived and eventually learned to eat on his own, as long as it was soft canned food.

The fifth week after the puppies' birth I placed an ad in the newspaper, and within a week we had people interested in all the pups—except the one with the deformity.

Late one afternoon I went to the store to pick up a few groceries. Upon returning I happened to see the old retired schoolteacher who lived across the street from us, waving at me. She had read in the paper that we had puppies and was wondering if she might get one from us for her grandson and his family. I told her all the puppies had found homes, but I would keep my eyes open for anyone else who might have an available cocker spaniel. I also mentioned that if someone should change their mind, I would let her know.

Within days all but one of the puppies had been picked up by their new families. This left me with one brown and tan cocker, as well as the smaller puppy with the cleft lip and palate.

Two days passed without my hearing anything from the gentleman who had been promised the tan and brown pup. I telephoned the schoolteacher and told her I had one puppy left and that she was welcome to come and look at him. She advised me that she was going to pick up her grandson and would come over at about eight o'clock that evening.

That night at around 7:30, Judy and I were eating supper when we heard a knock on the front door. When I opened the door, the man who had wanted the tan and brown pup was standing there. We walked inside, took care of the adoption details, and I handed him the puppy. Judy and I did not know what we would do or say when the teacher showed up with her grandson.

At exactly eight o'clock the doorbell rang. I

opened the door, and there was the school-teacher with her grandson standing behind her. I explained to her the man had come for the puppy after all, and there were no puppies left.

"I'm sorry, Jeffery. They found homes for all the puppies," she told her grandson.

Just at that moment, the small puppy left in the bedroom began to yelp.

"My puppy! My puppy!" yelled the little boy as he ran out from behind his grand-mother.

I just about fell over when I saw that the small child also had a cleft lip and palate. The boy ran past me as fast as he could, down the hallway to where the puppy was still yelping.

When the three of us made it to the bed-room, the small boy was holding the puppy in his arms. He looked up at his grandmother and said, "Look, Grandma. They found homes for all the puppies except the pretty one, and he looks just like me."

My jaw dropped in surprise.

The schoolteacher turned to us. "Is this puppy available?"

Recovering quickly, I answered, "Yes, that puppy is available."

The little boy, who was now hugging the puppy, chimed in, "My grandma told me these kind of puppies are real expensive and that I have to take real good care of it."

The lady opened her purse, but I reached over and pushed her hand away so that she would not pull her wallet out.

"How much do you think this puppy is worth?" I asked the boy. "About a dollar?"

"No. This puppy is very, very expensive," he replied.

"More than a dollar?" I asked.

"I'm afraid so," said his grandmother.

The boy stood there, pressing the small puppy against his cheek.

"We could not possibly take less than two dollars for this puppy," Judy said, squeezing my hand. "Like you said, it's the pretty one."

The schoolteacher took out two dollars and

handed it to the young boy.

"It's your dog now, Jeffery. You pay the man."

Still holding the puppy tightly, the boy proudly handed me the money. Any worries I'd had about the puppy's future were gone.

Although this happened many years ago, the image of the little boy and his matching pup stays with me still. I think it must be a wonderful feeling for any young person to look at themselves in the mirror and see nothing, except "the pretty one."

~Roger Dean Kiser

Scouting Out a Home

We didn't have the space or the energy to take in any more animals. Richard and I and our three dogs and three cats were already cramped in our small, rented home. The last year had brought the deaths of my father and grandmother, a move to a new city, the start of my career as a veterinarian, the purchase of our first house and plans for our wedding. I was exhausted and emotionally drained, which explains how Annie ended up at the shelter that first day.

Richard, a park-service employee, arrived at work to find two dogs—a young golden retriever and a small, black terrier—gallivanting around outside the old house in the woods that served as his office. Both dogs were very friendly, readily coming to him for an ear rub and a check of their collars. They didn't have any kind of identification, so Richard decided to give them a little time to see if they would head home on their own. For several hours he kept an eye on them through his window, but they showed no inclination to leave. The dogs could only get into trouble if they hung around for much longer, so Richard brought them into his office and called me at the veterinary clinic.

"Hi, honey, we've got a situation here." Richard went on to explain.

At the other end of the line, I groaned. "Look," I said. "The kennel is completely filled with patients and boarders, and we're still having trouble finding homes for our available adoptees. My boss will kill me if I let you bring them here, and you know that we can't handle any more dogs at home."

"Well, what do you think I should do?"

"The best place for them is probably the shelter," I replied, feeling a little frazzled. "If their owners want them back, that would be the first place they'd look."

Richard could tell I was in no mood for an argument and agreed to make the call to animal control. The officer told him that it would be afternoon before she could pick up the dogs. Several hours and a shared lunch later, Richard shepherded them out of his office and reluctantly handed them over.

That evening over dinner our conversation centered around the two dogs. Richard had grown attached to them in the short period of time that they had spent at his office. I was beginning to feel a little guilty for not trying harder to find a way to fit them in at the clinic. We concluded that we had probably done the right thing under the circumstances but hated to think about what the future could hold for the two good-natured dogs.

A week later I was wrapping up the morning appointments at the clinic when the receptionist called to the back, "Dr. Coates, there are two dogs waiting at the front door."

I sighed. *Walk-in appointments at one o'clock. There goes my lunch break.*

"Okay, Royann, please put them in room one and tell the owners that I'll be right in."

"No, Dr. C, you don't understand. It's just two dogs, no people, and now they're starting to head for the road."

"Go get them," I shrieked through the intercom as we all went running for the front door. The clinic is situated on a busy four-lane road that has been responsible for many of our trauma patients. Thankfully, before I could even make it past the reception area, Royann was steering the dogs through the front door. I stopped short. Before me was a golden retriever and a slightly scruffy black terrier.

"I may be crazy," I said "but I think these are the dogs that were at Richard's office last week." The clinic staff was aware of the story, and looks of disbelief passed all around. If these were the same dogs, what had happened to them at the shelter? I guessed that they had somehow escaped. But what were the chances that they could have found both Richard and me, in a town of thirty-four thousand people, when our offices are separated by five miles?

Needing to know if these were the same two dogs, I brought them home with me after work. As I pulled to a stop in the driveway, my own three dogs, Owen, Duncan and Boomer, sensed that I was not alone in the truck. The sounds of five dogs barking brought Richard to the kitchen door.

"Hey, babe," I hollered over the din. "I've got some folks here I think you might know."

He made his way to the back of the truck and peered through the fogged-up window of the shell. "What? How?" His stunned expression gave me my answer.

We let them out of the truck to investigate their new surroundings, and they scampered around the yard, tails wagging. I smiled with relief thinking how lucky they had been to escape harm during their recent escapades. The circumstances were too eerie to ignore, and Richard and I decided that they could stay with us until we figured out a long-term solution.

The next morning I left for work with the newcomers still in the fenced yard. Our three dogs stared forlornly out of the front windows of the house as I drove away. I promised to come back at lunch for some supervised introductions and play.

Returning home a few hours later, I could hear dogs barking but was a little surprised when nobody greeted me at the gate. As I pulled up to the kitchen door, I could hear that all the noise was coming from inside the house. A search of the yard proved that the gates were just as I had left them—the two dogs must have gone over the fence. My heart sank as I realized that they had vanished. We had been given a second chance to help, but now that opportunity was gone along with the dogs.

Several weeks passed, during which time we started moving to the farm that we had recently purchased in a nearby town. All our free time was spent traveling between the two houses to renovate and clean. Memories of the two itinerant dogs were beginning to fade, and I no longer expected to see them around every corner.

One Saturday morning, I began to pull away from the house with a load of boxes and furniture. I stopped the van at the base of the driveway and glanced to the left to check for traffic. In the distance I could just make out a small black dog trotting purposefully down the side of the road. Not wanting to get my hopes up, I slowly got out of the van for a closer look. As she got nearer, she picked up speed and ran to a stop in front of me. Jumping up, she put her front feet on my thighs and gave me a look as if to say, *I choose you.* This amazing little dog had somehow made her way back to us for the third time, and I was elated! But where was her friend? The two had been through so much together; I couldn't imagine that anything but the worst would have caused their separation.

Although Annie's friend never did return

to our home, he did show up again at the clinic a month later. I had no idea that this was going to be anything but a routine appointment. Walking into the exam room, I glanced at the chart—a golden retriever, one of our most popular breeds. I petted the high-spirited dog as I asked his new owner, "So how'd this beautiful boy come into your life?"

"It's a funny thing, Doc," she said. "He showed up at our house a couple times but always left within a day or two. He was hanging around with another dog, but when he came back to stay this last time he was alone."

I started to laugh as I finally recognized my old friend. Crouching in front of him for a more appropriate hello, I said to his new owner, "Let me guess: the other dog was about so high, shaggy and black with a gray muzzle."

Astonished, she asked, "How could you possibly know that?"

We compared our stories and were both

thrilled that, in the end, the two nomads had each found themselves a loving and permanent home.

~Jennifer Coates, D.V.M.

The Parking-Lot Dog

It was just a routine trip to the drugstore but it changed my life.

As I got out of my car, I noticed a scared, starving, mangy dog with rusty red fur in the store parking lot. He looked as though he was waiting for someone. I learned from a store clerk that a man in a pickup truck had dumped the dog in the parking lot and had driven away. Obviously this dog was waiting for the man's return. By the look in the dog's sad eyes, I knew he needed help.

For the next several days I returned to the drugstore parking lot and tried coaxing the dog with food. Like clockwork, the dog would appear from the woods but wouldn't approach the food until I drove away. I realized that if I were going to help this dog, I needed to use a humane trap. But the next day when I pulled into the lot with the humane trap in the car, the dog was gone. I searched the woods and the surrounding area, but the dog was nowhere to be found.

I decided to hang "Lost Dog" posters in the area. The only information I could put on the poster was a description of the red dog and my phone number. I didn't even know the dog's gender. I don't make a habit of rescuing dogs, and I already had two dogs of my own—why was I looking for a dog I knew nothing about? I couldn't explain it, but I was determined to find this dog.

Within a day I received a phone call from a clerk at a convenience store located about a mile from where I had first seen the dog. He said a red dog fitting the description on the poster had appeared at the convenience store and had been running up to pickup trucks in the parking lot. He explained that animal control had picked up the dog and had taken him to the county shelter. Although it was almost an hour away, I drove to the shelter to see if it was the same dog. There he was, crouched in the back corner of his cage growling, barking and very agitated. The shelter must hold dogs for ten days to allow owners time to claim them, so I would have to wait and see what happened with this dog.

Even though I had no plans of adding a third dog to our family, I felt compelled to help this dog. So over the next ten days I checked on him regularly. The people at the shelter told me the dog was very aggressive. They said no one would adopt him, and he would be destroyed when his time was up. On the tenth day I made the long drive back to the shelter to see the red dog. The receptionist asked if my name was Deborah Wood. I didn't pay much attention to her question; just simply replied "no" as I followed her back to the dog's cage. There was the red dog, just as scared and agitated as before.

Intimidated by the dog's behavior, but still determined to save him, I asked the kennel assistant to bring the dog out to my car and put him into the crate that I had brought for him. I had no idea if I would be able to handle the dog once we reached home, but I knew he couldn't stay at the shelter. As I followed the assistant and dog through the lobby area to my car, the receptionist stopped me. She said there was a Deborah Wood on the phone. She was inquiring about the red dog and wanted to speak to me.

I picked up the phone. The woman named Deborah told me that she had been at the convenience store talking to the clerk about the dog when animal control had picked him up. For some reason, she had been drawn to the red dog, too. Over the past ten days, Deborah had made several visits. She had tried coaxing the dog out of his cage for a walk, but the fearful dog had snapped at her. Despite the dog's behavior, Deborah never gave up on him, and now she wanted to know what I was going to

do with the dog. I explained to her that I was
taking the dog to the veterinarian for a
checkup and that I would call her once I got
home. It turned out that Deborah and I lived
within five minutes of each other. Both of us
had traveled almost an hour to visit the
"unadoptable" red dog at the shelter— both of
us not completely sure why. I was struck by
the lucky timing of her call. If Deborah had
called the shelter a moment later, we might
never have made a connection.

I was nervous about the dog being in my
car and anxious to get him to the vet. Surely I
would be able to figure out what to do with
him after that. *I must be crazy*, I thought, as I
backed my car out of the shelter's parking lot.
*Why am I doing this? I have an aggressive dog
crated in my car, and I have no idea what I'm going
to do with him.*

Just as I thought this, the red dog looked at
me with his expressive eyes and stuck his paw
through the crate for a "handshake." I reached
over and tentatively closed my hand around

the outstretched paw. It seemed to me that the red dog was thanking me. This melted my heart. I held his paw in my hand for the entire forty-five-minute ride to the vet's office. When we arrived, we were both smiling!

The red dog spent about two weeks at the vet's recovering from mange, worms and other health problems.

While the red dog was being treated at the vet's office, Deborah came often to visit him, and although she had never had a dog before, when the dog was well enough to leave the animal clinic, she offered to foster him until we could find him a permanent home. It didn't surprise anyone that Deborah quickly fell in love with her foster dog and decided to adopt him, naming him Redd. The moment Redd realized that he was safe, he became the perfect dog: affectionate and sociable—loving everyone he met. He never again showed any sign of aggression.

It has been five years since Deborah adopted Redd. Initially drawn together by our concern for Redd, Deborah and I have become close friends. And Redd has *two* families that adore him. He also frequently visits his "uncle," the clerk at the convenience store who responded to my poster.

Today, Redd is surrounded by people who love him. When I see this contented dog, lying on the sofa and getting belly rubs, I find it hard to believe that he is the same dog with the haunted eyes I saw in the parking lot five years ago. That routine trip to the drugstore brought a very special dog and a dear friend into my life.

~Wendy Kaminsky

The Promise

For the past twelve and a half years, I have been an animal control officer (ACO) for Polk County, Iowa. In this profession, you learn early on to toughen your skin, otherwise the stress and emotional drain that come with this job will bring you down. There have been a lot of dogs over the years that I would have loved to take home and make a part of my family, but in this line of work, it's not realistic to believe you can do that with each one—there are just too many dogs in need of good homes. Still, there is always that one that gets through your defenses. For me, that dog was Buddy.

Buddy was the most elusive dog I ever encountered in my years as an animal control

officer: I spent an amazing sixteen months trying to catch the big black dog.

I first received a phone call in November
2002 from a lady who said, "There is a dog
lying in a field near my home. He has been
there for a couple of days, and it is supposed
to get really cold tonight. Could you try to
catch him?" I told her I would head out there
and see what I could do.

As I drove up to the area, I could see that
the dog was lying on his side next to a small
hillside that served as a sort of break from the
cold wind. I got out of my truck with a leash
in hand and walked toward him. The dog was
asleep and did not hear my coming, so as I got
within twenty feet of him, I whistled because I
did not want to startle him. He immediately
got up and started barking at me. Then he
turned and ran away, into the middle of the
snow-covered field where he lay down to keep
a watchful eye on me. I knew there was going
to be no catching him that day, so I left to
answer another call that had come in.

That night it did get very cold. I just couldn't keep my mind off the black dog and wondered how he was doing out in that large, cold field all alone.

The next morning I headed to the Animal Rescue League of Iowa. This is where the county sheriff's department houses the animals I pick up, and it is the largest animal shelter in the state. I wanted to check the reports to see if anyone had called in saying they had lost their black dog. I hoped that someone was looking for this dog, so I would be able to ask the owners to come out to the field; I figured if it were their dog, the dog would come to them. There were no such lost reports.

On my way home that night, I couldn't help but drive by the field. There he sat, right in the middle of it. Again, he wouldn't let me get close to him or come to me when I called.

We played this game for a few weeks. I would get calls from different people reporting that a black dog was sitting in a field. I could not get this dog out of my mind, and even on my days off, I would drive by the field to leave food and see if I could get a look at him. He was always there, usually lying right out in the middle so no one would be able to sneak up behind him. I tried over and over to gain his trust with no luck. I could not get closer than a hundred yards from him—too far to use a tranquilizer dart. If I tried to come any closer, he would get up, bark and move to an adjacent field. I wondered sadly what could have happened to this dog to make him so fearful of people.

Finally, I spoke to Janet, one of the animal-care technicians at the Animal Rescue League. She had a reputation of being able to get close to dogs that would not let anyone near them. I told her about the black dog and asked her if she would try to catch him. She agreed, and she did try—to no avail.

It was now late December and the nights were very cold, dropping to ten or twenty degrees below zero. The woman who had called me originally about the dog continued to call, checking in to see what I was doing to help him. I assured her I had been trying to catch him and that I was leaving food for the dog. At this point I told her I was pondering a way to set a live trap to capture the dog. Privately, I worried how he would live through the nights given the bitter cold temperatures of Iowa winters.

The weeks passed. I checked on him regularly, driving by in the morning on my way to work, cruising by during the day and making my final round on my way home at night. It was odd—just seeing him out there made me smile. I was thankful he had made it through one more night and was still alive.

Janet and I talked constantly about this dog. A live trap hadn't worked. We simply could not come up with a way to catch this dog. One day we decided that we would take some shelter out to the fields, line it with blankets and put some food beside it; perhaps he would use it. We got an "igloo" type of doghouse and went out to the field to set it up. The dog watched us intently but wouldn't come near. That was the day that I named the dog Buddy. Looking at him, I made a promise to myself and to him: "Buddy, if I ever catch you, I'm going to adopt you and show you what 'good people' are like."

We went through the rest of the winter like this, as well as the following spring and summer. One day Buddy just seemed to vanish. No more sightings, no more concerned calls about him. I continued to think about him, fearing the worst: that he had been hit by a car and was no longer alive.

That fall, however, I received a call about a black dog standing by the road close to the field where I had first seen Buddy. I couldn't believe it. It had been seven months since I had last seen him, but I immediately hopped into my truck and drove to the area. There, standing by the road, was my friend Buddy. He looked just as he had the last time I saw him. I stopped my truck and got out. I tried to approach him, but as usual he started backing up and barking at me. This time, however, when I turned to walk away, instead of turning and running, he just sat down. He was letting me get closer.

We started the game all over again. I kept leaving treats for him in the same spot. This went on for months until one day he did something he hadn't done before—he slept next to the spot where I had been leaving his treats. I decided I would leave a live trap for him on that spot along with some barbecued pork. When I went back first thing the next morning, it looked like he'd tried to get the food out by digging around the trap, but he was nowhere to be seen.

I tried again the next night. This time I put a slice of pizza in the trap, hoping it would do the trick. I couldn't sleep that night and rose early to go check the cage. It was still dark out, and as I approached I heard Buddy bark. I figured he had heard me and was already retreating, but as I squinted my eyes I could make out the outline of a black dog caught in the cage of the live trap. Overwhelmed with relief and joy, I started to cry. Then I called my wife. "I got Buddy," I told her. "I got him!"

Buddy growled at me as I loaded the cage into my truck and drove to the Animal Rescue League. As I drove in, Janet was just coming into work. I yelled to her, "You are never going to guess who I've got!"

Janet replied, "Buddy?" and started to cry.

Janet and I unloaded the cage and took Buddy to a kennel. I crawled into the kennel with him, keeping my distance. Once I realized he wasn't going to bite me, I just started petting him and loving him. I spent the next few hours trying to build the bond that I knew would last a lifetime. To everyone's surprise, after running from us and being alone for sixteen months, he was a very affectionate dog. All Buddy wanted at this point was to be petted, and if you stopped too soon, he'd let you know by gently nuzzling your hand until you started petting him again.

Over the next few days, I spent almost

every free moment with Buddy. I would go to the Animal Rescue League before work, during lunch breaks and after work just so I could spend time with him. A few days later I brought my yellow Labrador, Hershey, to the shelter to meet Buddy. From the moment they met, they got along just fine.

Soon I was able to take Buddy home. Buddy fit amazingly well into our family. He had no "accidents" in the house and didn't destroy anything. Then one day my wife called me and told me that Buddy had gotten into the refrigerator. At first, I didn't believe her, but I suppose all that time scavenging for food had made him highly resourceful. Because it's true—I now live with a dog that can open a refrigerator!

We have to use bungee cords to prevent Buddy from opening the refrigerator door. There have been a few occasions when we have forgotten, only to come home to find that he's emptied the fridge. We've nicknamed him "Buddy, the Fridge King."

It's been four months now since I adopted him, and he is truly a bright spot in my life. I still can't believe this dog survived for sixteen months on his own, through two Iowa winters! He is an example of the true spirit and determination of the species we call "dog."

My long days at work are still challenging, but I am comforted by the thought that I get to go home and lavish Buddy with the love I wish all dogs could have. I kept my promise to Buddy and have shown him that people can be good. It was a happy ending worth waiting for.

~Bill King

Sled Dogs without Snow

One summer day my dogs and I were hiking along, making our way through the Cleveland Metro parks, when we came to a picnic area. Off to our left I saw several Port-O-Lets—those portable toilets shaped like telephone booths—and noticed that one was being used in a very unusual fashion.

Parked next to this particular Port-O-Let was a cart. It looked like some sort of sled-training cart with wheels used when there is no snow, but that was pure speculation on my part. In any case, the cart was not the unusual part. What was truly unusual were the four Siberian husky/Alaskan malamute–type dogs in harnesses, all hooked to one gang line that went directly into the door of the Port-O-Let, making it appear that they were out on a Port-O-Let/sled-riding mission. I can only assume there was no way to anchor the cart and the dogs while taking care of business, so the cart driver got the brilliant idea to just take the gang line into the Port-O-Let and hold on to the dogs while using the facilities.

Perhaps you're thinking the same thing I was thinking when I saw this little setup. I began fishing in my pack for my digital camera to take a picture of the "Port-O-Let-pulling team" when my dogs started yanking on their leashes, almost toppling me over. I looked around to see what in blazes had set them off.

It was a squirrel that had decided to stop in the middle of the wide-open field to my left, pick up a nut and chew on it. The problem was that my three dogs and the four Port-O-Let-anchored sled dogs were hanging out in the very same field. So far the potty chain gang hadn't seen the squirrel, but it was only a matter of time as my dogs were doing the if-we-

weren't-on-this-leash-we-would-kick-that-squirrel's-butt dance with increasing intensity.

Sure enough, within seconds, the potty-pullers' heads all snapped in the direction of my dogs, then in the direction of the squirrel. They appeared to have the same idea as my pack, who were still straining vigorously at their leashes. At that point, my dogs saw the sled dogs spot the squirrel, and some sort of dog tribal-hunting, nonverbal communication thing happened: every one of the seven dogs on either end of the field realized that it was a race to see which of the two groups could get to the squirrel first. My dogs redoubled their pulling efforts, and the four-dog sled team reacted as one, barking furiously and lunging full steam for the squirrel.

The dogs' motion caused the Port-O-Let to spin about thirty degrees and rock like the dickens. Luckily it didn't tip over, just teetered back and forth a time or two, then righted itself. But nothing was going to stop the sled team in their pursuit of the squirrel. They gave another huge yank. The Port-O-Let spun yet again, and from inside the green tower of potty privacy came a human screech, finally piercing through the dogs' din. The screech had the immediate effect of slowing the port-o-pullers down, and they settled into a nervous stand.

Unfortunately, at this point, the squirrel realized that my dogs weren't going to get him, and the port-o-pullers *couldn't* get him, so he started doing some kind of nah-nah-nah-nah-nah-you-can't-get-me dance, once more infuriating the port-o-pullers and driving my dogs crazy.

If you've ever wondered why dogsleds are built long and low to the ground, as opposed to square and tall—like, say, the shape of a Port-O-Let—you needn't wonder any longer whether this is a design flaw. When the pulling and barking started up again, the Port-O-Let did its best to stay upright, rocking heavily back and forth. The dogs, sensing victory, forgot completely about the squirrel and started timing their pulls with the rocking. They gave one last enormous tug and yanked the Port-O-Let over. Toppling the tall green box seemed to give the dog team a sense of satisfaction; they immediately stopped pulling after the Port-O-Let crashed to the ground. The squirrel had finally gone, and with the dogs quiet, I could now hear a series of cusswords coming from the fallen Port-O-Let.

I figured I'd better head over that way and see if I could help. Sadly, the Port-O-Let had landed facedown, meaning the door was now the bottom—against the ground. I tied my dogs to a tree and ventured closer. I asked if the occupant of the tipped Port-O-Let was okay. A woman's voice said yes—actually, she used far more colorful language, but for the purpose of this story, we'll just say she said yes.

The Port-O-Let hadn't fared as well. You could tell it was badly hurt because there was a lot of blue fluid leaking from it. I told the woman that I would have to roll the Port-O-Let on its side so we could try opening the door, and that she should find something to hang on to. A couple of good shoves later, the Port-O-Let rolled 90 degrees, exposing the door. The door opened and out crawled Mama Smurf. The poor woman was covered in the blue "blood" of the dying Port-O-Let.

Her dogs came running over and decided she needed a bath, which did not make her at all happy. At this point, she suddenly realized she had skipped Step 10 in the bathroom process—pull your pants up—and with a yelp, she quickly disappeared back into the Port-O-Let to finish. When she reappeared, she was in absolutely no mood to talk about her ride on the wild side (I didn't blame her), so I told her the short version of what happened outside the Port-O-Let.

I helped her hook her dogs up to the cart, and off she went, glowing blue as she drove down the path and back into the Metro park woods. I had to laugh imagining the reactions of all the other people walking serenely through the park as they were passed by an irate Smurf and her merry band of blue-tongued dogs.

~Dave Wiley

Meet Our Contributors

Meghan Beeby is a full-time campaign coordinator for Farm Sanctuary, the nation's leading nonprofit farm animal protection organization: www.farmsanctuary.org. She lives in Ithaca, New York, with her husband, John, and twenty-seven companion animals. Meghan is also an active volunteer for human social service organizations. Her e-mail is: meghanbeeby@hotmail.com.

Jennifer Coates graduated from the Virginia-Maryland Regional College of Veterinary Medicine as valedictorian in 1999 and has practiced small animal medicine ever since. She lives with her husband, dogs, cats and horses in western Wyoming and is currently writing a veterinary dictionary for animal owners. Please contact her at: *jencoates@silverstar.com*.

Elisabeth Ann Freeman is an award-winning writer and speaker. She resides in Michigan with her husband, John, and four children. She attends Mount Hope Church in Ovid and serves in youth ministry. She has two books and over eighty articles/stories published. Please e-mail her at: *writeforlife@ charter.net* or log on to her Web site: *http://writeforlife.com*.

Christine Henderson lives in Minnesota with her husband, their three children and two Brittanys. She recently became a stay-at-home mom and works as a freelance writer in her spare time.

Wendy Kaminsky is a software analyst at Dominion Virginia Power. Wendy enjoys traveling, running and working with animals. She and her husband, Dennis, volunteer at a local animal shelter. Through their rescue efforts they have adopted three dogs and two cats who are loved and spoiled beyond words.

Bill King has been an animal control officer for twelve years. Bill enjoys the outdoors, travel and his career. When you're looking for your new pet, consider your local animal shelter.

Roger Dean Kiser's stories have been published in seventeen books in five countries. Roger will never forget he was treated as though he was less than human while living in a Jacksonville, Florida, orphanage. Roger's story can be found at: *www.geocities.com/trampolineone/survive/noframe.htm*. Contact Roger at: *trampolineone@webtv.net*.

When not barricading his home against his ravenous dog, **Sam Minier** spends his free time in more lighthearted pursuits—writing horror stories and poetry! Brave souls can sample his work at: *www.samuelminier.com*.

Micki Ruiz lives in South Florida with her husband, Steve. A published author, she writes short stories and historical fiction, and is (still) hard at work on her novel, a fantasy adventure. This is her first nonfiction work. Please e-mail her at: *LadySunshine817@yahoo.com*

Dave Wiley is an information technology professional who enjoys just about anything. He likes taking on Tim-the-Toolman-like projects while achieving similar results, playing with his son, camping, hiking with the dogs, performing confirmation and obedience events with the dogs, and generally just doing stuff that helps him to avoid any type of house-cleaning. He is hoping to become a writer someday when he grows up. He can be reached by e-mail at: *wiley@mayfran.com.*

Meet Our Authors

Jack Canfield is the co-creator of the *Chicken Soup for the Soul* series, which *Time* magazine has called "the publishing phenomenon of the decade." Jack is also the coauthor of many other bestselling books.

Jack is the CEO of the Canfield Training Group in Santa Barbara, California, and founder of the Foundation for Self-Esteem in Culver City, California. He has conducted intensive personal and professional development seminars on the principles of success for more than a million people in twenty-three countries, has spoken to hundreds of thousands of people at more than 1,000 corporations, universities, professional conferences and conventions, and has been seen by millions more on national television shows.

Jack has received many awards and honors,

including three honorary doctorates and a Guinness World Records Certificate for having seven books from the *Chicken Soup for the Soul* series appearing on the *New York Times* bestseller list on May 24, 1998.

You can reach Jack at
www.jackcanfield.com.

Mark Victor Hansen is the co-founder of Chicken Soup for the Soul, along with Jack Canfield. He is a sought-after keynote speaker, bestselling author, and marketing maven. Mark's powerful messages of possibility, opportunity, and action have created powerful change in thousands of organizations and millions of individuals worldwide.

Mark is a prolific writer with many bestselling books in addition to the *Chicken Soup for the Soul* series. Mark has had a profound influence in the field of human potential through his library of audios, videos, and articles in the areas of big thinking, sales achievement, wealth building, publishing success, and personal and professional development. He is also the founder of the MEGA Seminar Series.

Mark has received numerous awards that honor his entrepreneurial spirit, philanthropic heart, and business acumen. He is a lifetime member of the Horatio Alger Association of Distinguished Americans.

You can reach Mark at
www.markvictorhansen.com.

What Jacques Cousteau did for the oceans, what Carl Sagan did for space, **Dr. Marty Becker** is doing for pets.

As a veterinarian, author, university educator, media personality and pet lover, Dr. Becker is one of the most widely recognized animal health authorities in the world. He is also passionate about his work, fostering the affection-connection between pets and people that we call, "The Bond."

Marty coauthored *Chicken Soup for the Pet Lover's Soul, Chicken Soup for the Cat & Dog Lover's Soul, Chicken Soup for the Horse Lover's Soul* and *The Healing Power of Pets,* which was awarded a prestigious silver award in the National Health Information Awards.

Dr. Becker has powerful media platforms, including seven years as the popular veterinary contributor to ABC-TV's *Good Morning America*. Dr. Becker authors two highly regarded newspaper columns that are internationally distributed by Knight Ridder Tribune (KRT) Services. And in association with the American Animal Hospital Association (AAHA), Dr. Becker hosts a nationally syndicated radio program, *Top Vet Talk Pets* on the Health Radio Network.

Dr. Becker has been featured on *ABC, NBC, CBS, CNN, PBS, Unsolved Mysteries* and in *USA Today, The New York Times, The Washington Post, Reader's Digest, Forbes, Better Homes & Gardens, The Christian Science Monitor, Woman's Day, National Geographic Traveler, Cosmopolitan, Glamour, Parents* and major Web sites such as *ABCNews.com, Amazon.com, Prevention.com, Forbes.com* and *iVillage.com.*

The recipient of many awards, Dr. Becker holds one especially dear. In 2002, the Delta Society and the American Veterinary Medical Association (AVMA) presented Dr. Becker with the prestigious Bustad Award, as the Companion Animal Veterinarian of the Year for the United States.

Marty and his family enjoy life in northern Idaho and share Almost Heaven Ranch with two dogs, five cats and five quarter horses.

Contact Marty Becker at:

P.O. Box 2775

Twin Falls, ID 83303

Phone: 208-734-8174

Web site: *www.drmartybecker.com*

Carol Kline is passionate about cats! In addition to being a doting "pet parent," she is active in animal rescue work. Although she has recently relocated to California, she is still a member of the board of directors of the Noah's Ark Animal Foundation, *www.noahsark.org,* located in Fairfield, Iowa, a limited-access, "cageless," no-kill shelter that rescues lost, stray and abandoned dogs and cats. For the last eight years, Carol has spent many hours a week monitoring the fate of dogs and cats at Noah's Ark and working to find them good permanent homes. She also administered the Caring Community Spay/Neuter Assistance Program (CCSNAP), a fund especially designated for financially assisting pet owners to spay and neuter their pets. "The reward of helping these animals is more fulfilling than any paycheck I could ever receive.

Volunteering time with the animals fills my heart and brings great joy to my life."

A freelance writer/editor for nineteen years, Carol, who has a B.A. in literature, has written for newspapers, newsletters and other publications. In addition to her own *Chicken Soup* books, she has also contributed stories and her editing talents to many other books in the *Chicken Soup for the Soul* series.

In addition to her writing and animal work, Carol is a motivational speaker and gives presentations to animal-welfare groups around the country on a variety of topics. She has also taught stress-management techniques to the general public since 1975.

Carol has the good fortune to be married to Larry and is a proud stepmother to Lorin, twenty-three, and McKenna, twenty. She has three dogs—all rescues—Beau, Beethoven and Jimmy.

To contact Carol, write to her at:

P.O. Box 521

Ojai, CA 93024

E-mail: *ckline@lisco.com*

Amy D. Shojai is an animal behavior consultant, award-winning author, lecturer, and a nationally known authority on pet care and behavior. She is a passionate proponent of owner education in her books, articles, columns and media appearances, and has been recognized by her peers as "one of the most authoritative and thorough pet reporters."

The former veterinary technician has been a full-time pet journalist for more than two decades. She is a member of the International Association of Animal Behavior Consultants and consults with a wide range of animal care professionals, researchers and other experts, and specializes in translating "medicalese" into easily understood jargon- free language to make it accessible to all pet lovers. Amy answers pet questions in her weekly "Emotional Health" column at *www.catchow.com*, hosts "Your Pet's Well-Being with Amy Shojai" at *iVillage.com* and is section leader for the Holistic and Behavior/Care portions of the PetsForum. She is also the author of twenty-one nonfiction pet books, including *PETiquette: Solving Behavior Problems in Your Multipet Household* and *Complete Care for Your Aging Dog,* and a coauthor of *Chicken Soup for the Cat Lover's Soul.*

In addition to writing and pet care consulting, Amy's performance background (B.A. in music and theater) aids in her media work as a corporate spokesperson and pet product consultant. She has appeared on *Petsburgh USA/Disney* Channel Animal Planet series, *Good Day New York, Fox News: Pet News, NBC Today Show* and made hundreds of radio appearances including *Animal Planet Radio.* Amy has been featured in *USA Weekend, The New York Times, The Washington Post, Reader's Digest, Woman's Day, Family Circle, Woman's World,* as well as the "pet press." As a founder and president emeritus of the Cat Writers' Association, a member of the Dog Writers Association of America and the Association of Pet Dog Trainers, her work has been honored with over two dozen writing awards from these and many other organizations.

Amy and her husband, Mahmoud, live among 700-plus antique roses and assorted critters at Rosemont, their thirteen-acre "spread" in north Texas.

To contact Amy, write to her at:
P.O. Box 1904
Sherman, TX 75091
E-mail: *amy@shojai.com*
Web site: *www.shojai.com*

Chicken Soup for the Soul
Improving Your Life Every Day

Real people sharing real stories—for twenty years. Now, Chicken Soup for the Soul has gone beyond the bookstore to become a world leader in life improvement. Through books, movies, DVDs, online resources and other partnerships, we bring hope, courage, inspiration and love to hundreds of millions of people around the world. Chicken Soup for the Soul's writers and readers belong to a one-of-a-kind global community, sharing advice, support, guidance, comfort, and knowledge.

Chicken Soup for the Soul stories have been translated into more than forty languages and can be found in more than one hundred countries. Every day, millions of people experience a Chicken Soup for the Soul story in a book, magazine, newspaper or online. As we share our life experiences through these stories, we offer hope, comfort and inspiration to one another. The stories travel from person to person, and from country to country, helping to improve lives everywhere.

Share with Us

We all have had Chicken Soup for the Soul moments in our lives. If you would like to share your story or poem with millions of people around the world, go to chickensoup.com and click on "Submit Your Story." You may be able to help another reader, and become a published author at the same time. Some of our past contributors have launched writing and speaking careers from the publication of their stories in our books!

Our submission volume has been increasing steadily—the quality and quantity of your submissions has been fabulous. We only accept story submissions via our website. They are no longer accepted via mail or fax.

To contact us regarding other matters, please e-mail webmaster@chickensoupforthesoul.com, or fax or write us at:

Chicken Soup for the Soul
P.O. Box 700
Cos Cob, CT 06807-0700
Fax: 203-861-7194

One more note from your friends at Chicken Soup for the Soul: Occasionally, we receive an unsolicited book manuscript from one of our readers, and we would like to respectfully inform you that we do not accept unsolicited manuscripts and we must discard the ones that appear.